INSPIRING STORIES FOR AWESOME GIRLS

A MOTIVATIONAL COLLECTION OF STORIES ABOUT COURAGE, SELF-CONFIDENCE AND FRIENDSHIP

SOPHIE MILLER

ISBN: 979-8-88768-000-2

CONTENTS

Introduction.. 1

Shelly At The Skating Rink... 3

    Moral Of The Story 10

Bella's Birthday Bash 11

    Moral Of The Story 17

A Circle Of Friends 19

    Moral Of The Story 27

Major Math Mishap 29

    Moral Of The Story 35

Planet Presentations.. 37

    Moral Of The Story 42

Losing A Best Friend 43

    Moral Of The Story 51

Dinner At Pal's Pizza 53

Moral Of The Story 60

Molly's Speech...61

Moral Of The Story 68

Gardening Goals 69

Moral Of The Story 76

A Night On Stage...77

Moral Of The Story 82

Conclusion 83

INTRODUCTION

Life in today's world is busy, full of worries, and courage isn't always easy to find, especially for children. With school problems, homework, friends, and life changes, young girls have a lot to handle. Aside from these types of issues, there are a ton of joyful days ready to be celebrated as well.

Sometimes, life just feels like a giant roller coaster. At times it's full of excitement, sometimes it's a letdown, other times it's amazing, and every so often, it's frightening. With so much wisdom needed and so many things to learn, it may seem like there aren't enough hours in a day to understand the life lesson in every event.

An important piece of advice is to look for value in everything that happens in life. Try to learn from every choice you make and use it to help yourself and others in the future. Even if a mistake or a bad choice is made, there

1

is always a concept of truth you can gain from any adventure you encounter.

The stories in this book are written to share real life problems in the lives of young girls. In each story, there's a moral to understand, and through the actions of each character, their fears and concerns are resolved.

There are examples of encouragement in each story, and they are meant to build self-esteem and mindfulness, while teaching bravery, strength, and determination.

SHELLY AT THE
SKATING RINK

Friday afternoon was quickly passing, and all Shelly could
think about was the next day. She wasn't looking forward

to the trip to the roller-skating rink at all. One of her friends, Tina, was having a sleepover and for fun, her mother was treating them to an evening of skating. After that, they planned on roasting hot dogs and marshmallows in Tina's backyard.

For most girls, that sounds like a blast. But, for Shelly, it was worrying her to the top level. She had never been skating before but was scared that if she told her friends, they would laugh and make fun of her. She had read books where the characters knew how to skate, and she had seen television shows where the actors were great at skating. In real life, though, she had no idea what it felt like to slip on those silly-looking, lace-up shoes with wheels on the bottom. She already had enough trouble not tripping in her real shoes! How in the world would she handle *rolling on wheels*?

Shelly was somewhat confident in herself most of the time. However, she had accepted a long time ago that she wasn't as popular as some of the other girls, and she sure wasn't as talented. One girl in her class was in a competition cheer squad that advanced to state level last year. Another already had her own dog-sitting business, and her best friend Marla always has the best grades in class. She couldn't compare to any of that. As plain as Shelly saw herself to be, she was okay with it. She just didn't want to add anything more to make her look worse—especially in front of all her friends!

In addition to worrying about looking crazy trying to skate, she knew falling would hurt...a lot. The thought of some pain and a few bruises wasn't terrible, but it had crossed her mind that she might break a bone. After seeing her brother fall from the treehouse one day and break his leg, she couldn't help but imagine herself in the same condition.

Jacob, her older brother, was in their treehouse last year and fell just as he began to climb down the ladder. Her mom and dad saw what happened and rushed him to the emergency room. Shelly's grandmother lived next door and stepped over to watch her until they returned. For the following six weeks, Jacob didn't have much pain, but he was stuck in a cast that was heavy, hot, and always seemed to be in his way.

As Shelly sat and remembered those days in her mind, she realized that even more time had passed, and that the sleepover was getting closer and closer. As she considered what she might do to get out of going to Tina's with all the rest of her friends, her mom called her down for dinner. She quickly snapped out of her thoughts when she realized her favorite meal was waiting in the kitchen. Her mother had made orange chicken with rice, beans, and cheesy vegetables. Not only did she forget about skating for a second, but she also noticed how hungry she was.

Shelly's dad, brother, and mom were already seated at the table when she entered the room. As she took her seat, her father asked about her day, and they began to discuss her grades in math. Meanwhile, Mom and Jacob talked about weekend plans. Since Shelly was going to the sleepover, her brother was allowed to have two friends spend the night at their house. He had planned a night of movies, swimming, and video games. Shelly didn't find video games all that fun, but they sure did sound better than skating. Why couldn't she just stay home? Skipping the sleepover wouldn't be so bad, right? Maybe she could act sick or pretend like she had a lot of homework for that weekend.

After dinner, she helped with the dishes and put away the leftovers. Her mother usually had to ask Shelly to do a little extra in the kitchen, so she was a bit surprised when she worked so hard without being asked. Mom also noticed that other than talking about math at the dinner table, Shelly had been rather quiet.

Once things were all settled after their meal, it was getting close to bedtime for everyone. Even though it was Friday, they all agreed not to stay up too late because Saturday mornings were what Mom called "yard day." In the spring and summer, the whole family worked together to keep the lawn looking good. They weeded, planted, raked, and mowed every weekend.

It was hard work and took a ton of effort, but they always seemed to have a great time. Who would think that pulling grass and sweating could be enjoyable? But Shelly and her family liked it!

That particular Saturday morning, Mom noticed that Shelly was still sort of quiet. She was concerned something may be wrong and decided to speak to her about it. As she asked her about things, Shelly's eyes filled up with tears the size of the tulips and she had just sat down. Right away, her mom pulled her close and hugged her tightly.

Through her tears, she tried to explain why she was crying. Although her mother could barely understand her, she did hear the words "skate," "Tina," and "scared." It didn't take her mom long to realize what was upsetting Shelly so much.

For the next half hour, they discussed the sleepover and Shelly's fears. Mom understood her feelings and talked her through her worries. She explained that Tina and the other girls were great friends to Shelly and that true friends would never laugh and make fun of someone, especially on their first try at something new.

So, together they came up with a plan to make the rest of the weekend happy and tear-free. Shelly's mother would explain her fears upon arriving at Tina's, and if anyone did happen to laugh or joke about Shelly's concerns, her mother would be there for comfort.

At 3:00 p.m. that afternoon, Mom and Shelly arrived at Tina's house across town. They were greeted at the door by Tina's mother and a group of loud, giggling girls. After everyone said hi and exchanged hugs, it was time to set their plan into action.

Shelly's mother took a minute to explain that Shelly had never been skating and was very excited to try something new. She asked the girls if they would guide Shelly and maybe teach her a few tricks if they knew any. As it turned out, three other girls had never been skating before either! Boy was Shelly relieved to hear that, and at that moment, her fears were erased.

At the skating rink that evening, as she laced up those silly-looking shoes with wheels, Shelly felt braver than she ever had before! She was a little wobbly for the first few rounds, but as she kept going, she got better and better. Overall, Shelly had a blast that night!

Moral of the story:

As Shelly realized that she was about to face some of her biggest fears, she became so worried that it showed in her actions and her mother could see it on her face. She learned, after talking with her mom, that sometimes things aren't as bad as you may believe. She was able to face her fears with a plan and with sympathetic understanding from a parent. Once she realized that worries aren't always what they seem, bravery took over, and Shelly had a great time skating.

BELLA'S BIRTHDAY BASH

It was only nine days until Bella's eighth birthday. She was more excited than she had ever been and could hardly wait for all her friends to arrive at her party. Everyone was going to have so much fun. She had been close to all of her friends since they started school four years ago.

They knew what kind of songs she liked, what foods were her favorites, and what she enjoyed doing outside of school. She and her friends shared an amazing bond, and Bella had every reason to believe that this year's party would be her biggest and best celebration yet!

Day by day, the time drew closer to her party, and her excitement grew with every minute. Not only was Bella's party going to have all the ordinary birthday magic, but she and her mom had also planned to set up an outdoor adventure park at their house! Her friends were in for a treat because that part was a surprise for them.

With just three days left until party time, Bella and her mother spent the afternoon choosing where to set up each station in the backyard. They sorted all the supplies into groups.

The water buckets and balloons for the water balloon station were set together near the outside faucet. The golf clubs and balls were placed where the mini-golf area would be, and the hula hoop station was supplied with four glittery hoops streaming with ribbons. Things were beginning to look great!

In addition to these stations, there were bean bags and targets to set up, and a few more activities they would take care of the next day. As Bella walked in with Mom for the evening, she mentioned that she wasn't very good at mini-golf, and she was afraid she would lose every time she played. Mom quickly reminded her that she may not win every game during her party, and just because she was the birthday girl, didn't mean she was expected to win.

Then her mother asked a question that made Bella start thinking. She asked how her friends would feel if Bella won every game and they were never the winners. That made Bella think to herself deeply and understand that if her friends never won at any of the games, the party may not seem like much fun to them. Her mom explained that for everyone to enjoy the night, each girl should feel successful at something.

So, the next afternoon, Bella went to her mother with some new ideas to add to the party. She showed her a list of things that she wasn't so great at, but her friends were, like jumping on one foot, doing cartwheels, and running relay races. She explained that she wanted the other girls to feel successful like her mom said, so they should include stations she knew her friends would enjoy.

She was certain that Maddi was great at hopping on one foot, and Lizzy was super at running relay races. Bella had also seen Emily's cartwheels. They were the best on the playground at school! After Mom listened to Bella, she smiled and gave her a huge bear hug.

Mom was so proud of Bella for learning such an important lesson about herself. She could see her daughter understood the true meaning of friendship. Bella had learnt she wasn't as good at some things as others are, and with other activities, she may be better. Whoever won the games didn't matter as long as the night turned out fun for everyone.

When Friday arrived, the party was set up and ready to go. Mom and Bella had worked to get everything just right, and the girls were all supposed to arrive at Bella's by 5:00 p.m. When coming in from school that afternoon, Bella put her bag in her room and went right to the backyard. Everything still looked great and was ready to go.

Finally, with just minutes left before arrival time, while Mom was in the kitchen preparing snacks and drinks, Bella was sitting on the front porch steps outside. She waited with excitement, and as she watched the first car pull up, she jumped up to greet her first guest. It was Emily!

Emily carried her bag, a gift wrapped in striped paper, and a sleeping bag with kittens on it. Both girls ran inside the house, giggling with joy. Mom watched with happiness and knew it was going to be such a fun night for the girls.

Next to arrive were Maddi, Sarah, and Lizzy. By 5:10 p.m., all the guests had arrived, and Bella's mother sat them all down on the floor of the living room to talk about the evening. In total, there were seven girls, including Bella.

She explained that they would put away all their things in Bella's room and then head to the backyard. Once they got there, they would need to line up next to the big oak tree near the table and chairs.

So, the girls got busy doing what she said. They were all wondering what was waiting by the tree and were so happy, with lots of whispering and big smiles. They had no idea what they were about to see!

As they all got in line, their eyes were big with disbelief. They had no idea that Bella and her mother had done so much work! It looked wonderful! Altogether, there were ten stations, and each one had a sign with a title for the activity and lots of decorations.

The cartwheel center was covered in ribbons and bows, the basketball area was decorated with orange and black streamers, and the mini-golf course had paper lanterns hanging above it from tree branches. Bella could see that her birthday bash was going to be a hit.

Throughout the evening, the girls played, had refreshments, and enjoyed themselves. Each guest had a chance to feel successful, and they agreed that a backyard play park was a terrific idea for a birthday party. They even asked Bella if she would have this kind of party every year.

At last, it was time to go in for dinner, presents, and cake. The girls made their way into the house and sat down at the table. Seeing all of her friends with smiles made Bella so happy. As she blew out her candles and the girls sang the 'Happy Birthday' song, Bella made a wish that every birthday could be as happy as this one!

Moral of the story:

A little girl, Bella, learns that she may not be great at some things, but she is great at others. You don't have to be the winner every time, just trying your best is what matters. Your friends' successes are as equally important as yours, especially when it comes to an event similar to Bella's party. She realized that it was important to include activities where her friends could win. Once she realized that it was perfectly okay for her to not be the best at every competition, her heart opened to the idea that she should celebrate when someone else was the best.

A CIRCLE OF FRIENDS

While making a list of things she needed to pack for summer camp, Jessie relaxed in front of the T.V. She thought about how camp was always fantastic and so full of activities. She had gone three years in a row, and this year would be the fourth.

Each year, she met new friends, got a chance to participate in a ton of outdoor sports, and learned more and more about teamwork. Summer camp was a valuable experience for everyone who attended.

This year would be different though. Over spring break, Jessie's parents got a divorce. Wow, had that really changed things in their home! Mom was sad all the time, and her little brother, Andy, was always with their dad. The entire family was in pieces, and Jessie felt helpless. There was absolutely no way camp would be as enjoyable. Maybe she shouldn't even go…

About the time Jessie decided to give up on her list, at least for a while, her m om came in with a bag of groceries. She asked Jessie to help out and get the rest out of the car. Jessie did as she was asked. While she was outside, her neighbor Callie, stopped by to say hi. Callie was a grade below Jessie in school, but they were good friends. They had been neighbors for about three years, and they often spent the night together.

While visiting, Callie mentioned summer camp. She always attended the same camp Jessie did and sort of looked to Jessie as a guide or mentor while they were there. Because Jessie was a year older, Callie felt comfortable sticking close to her during that week. Callie would always get a little homesick, and so many new people always made her feel nervous. But, because she had Jessie by her side, everything always turned out okay.

During their conversation, Jessie realized that if she didn't go, Callie wouldn't have her support and encouragement. She didn't want Callie to be uneasy and anxious during camp without her, but she truly was thinking about just staying home this year. If she did decide not to go, how on earth would she ever tell Callie? It would upset her very much.

After a few minutes of talking, Callie had to get back home for dinner and Jessie went inside with the groceries. Once she set the bags down to unload them, her mother began to talk about a trip that she had to take for work. Sometimes her mother was required to travel for her job. It didn't happen often, but when it did, it was never a problem because she and Andy would just stay home with Dad.

21

However, since the divorce, things were different in their lives. With Dad living two towns away, Jessie didn't get to see him as much as she wanted to, and she sure did miss him. It wouldn't be as easy to stay home with Dad if Dad wasn't even home!

But, before Jessie could ask her mother about staying with Dad during the trip, her mom said the trip was scheduled for the same week as Jessie's summer camp.

Mom thought it was great that they were scheduled for the same week. Then she told Jessie that she and Dad had talked, and they agreed it was time for Andy to begin going to camp also. She said when Andy found out, he shouted with excitement! There was absolutely no question now. Jessie knew there was no getting out of camp this year.

Once school was out a few weeks later, Jessie could feel the butterflies in her stomach each time she thought about summer camp. How would she have fun? What could she talk about with the girls there that wouldn't remind her of things at home?

She felt so unsure about so many things. However, there was one thing she was certain of. Camp would be hard and frustrating. While everyone would expect her to be happy, active, and win the 20-yard dash like she did every other year, she would be sitting in the cabin unhappy, waiting to go back home. Why did life have to be so difficult sometimes?

Finally, the day came to leave for camp. Dad brought Andy to Mom and Jessie's house, so he could tell Mom goodbye for the week. Andy gave Mom lots of hugs and seemed totally cool with heading out for camp.

That was very much the opposite of what was going on inside of Jessie. Not only did she have a very hard time saying goodbye to both parents, but she even cried! They both found it odd that she was crying, but she told them it was really no big deal. She said she was just worried about missing them.

After the last hugs, Mom took Jessie and Andy to camp while Dad went to work. She walked to the main office with the kids and helped to get them settled in. Next, she headed to the airport for her trip.

Not long after they arrived, Callie showed up and was assigned to the same cabin as Jessie. With her bags and two board games, Callie ran to Jessie in excitement! Right away, she started making plans for what they would do that first afternoon. Callie was great at bug hunting, and she had brought buckets with lids for each of them for collecting.

Within the next few minutes, two more girls arrived who were both assigned to the cabin with Jessie and Kelly. They spent the first hour or so getting to know each other, unpacking, and choosing which bed belonged to who. Both new girls seemed nice enough, but Jessie still wasn't feeling great about having to be there.

After a relaxing bug hunt, the campers were called to the dining hall for dinner. While they were eating, a few more girls joined them, and they all began talking about tomorrow's plans. Even though Jessie was sure this whole week was going to be a bummer, she was happy to see spaghetti and salad for dinner. That was her favorite meal at home. Jessie thought to herself that maybe there would be some good things about this week.

At the end of two full days of camp, Jessie had explored a mystery cave, played volleyball, bug hunted, made clay crafts, learned three nature songs, and made a woven basket. She had also spent lots of time in her cabin thinking about things back home. Why couldn't life always be easy? Why couldn't it just be fun and easy all the time?

The next day the campers went kayaking with their camp counselor. It was better than Jessie expected, but what she was worried about was the campfire talks that were coming that night. Every year, on the third night of camp, all the children sat around the campfire, made smores, and talked about, well, everything.

Whatever was on their mind, they could discuss. Some talked about their friends back home and some talked about their families. For others, it was something different. She was worried about what she should say.

She wasn't good at sharing her personal stories, but the campfire talks were perfect for that. Should she go ahead, in front of all those people, and talk about her parents? Well, she was about to find out. The campfire talks were only minutes away, and Jessie couldn't make up her mind about what to say.

When they walked up to the campfire area, the camp counselors already had a few smores made for the campers, and Jessie grabbed one. Smores were one of the best things about camp!

As she took the first bite, the camp leader began the talks by telling a story about her neighbor becoming sick with cancer. Then another leader spoke about a family vacation that he took the week before camp.

Finally, after several kids took a turn, Jessie decided to go through with it. She talked about everything she was going through, how it was affecting everyone in her family, and how she felt there was nothing she could do to help. She cried while she talked, but in the end, she got lots of hugs and support.

She realized how great the other children were being and she thanked them for being so kind. They all reminded her that the campfire talks were simply a circle of friends, sharing what they needed to share, while being supportive and encouraging to everyone else.

For the rest of camp, Jessie was filled with happiness and was relieved to have her worries gone. In the end, she looked back at a great week, and was glad she had attended summer camp for the fourth year in a row. As a matter of fact, she was already looking forward to next year!

Moral of the story:

Jessie was having a hard time dealing with things at home and how she was feeling about them. She was worried about summer camp and having to share those feelings with the other campers. In the end, she ends up choosing to share her problems and talk about them with others. Once she did, she realized how helpful it was to have others there to lean on in times of need.

MAJOR MATH MISHAP

Jana, a student who loved reading, wasn't so fond of math. Overall, she was a wonderful student. Her teachers always wrote positive notes home to her mother, she was kind and helpful during class, and she always tried her best. However, no matter how hard she worked, she was not very successful in her math class.

One day, while she was finishing up her last bit of double-digit subtraction, her teacher announced that there would be a test in two days. It would be about what they had learned during the past three weeks. Jana could feel her cheeks get red and she suddenly became very sweaty.

She had struggled the past three weeks in math more than she had all year. In addition to this double-digit subtraction, they had also begun working on multiplication factors. For most of her friends, this was no big deal. But for Jana, it was terrible.

That evening after school, Jana went to dance class like she did every Wednesday. She had practiced her routines all week and knew them well. When she stepped up to show the teacher how much she had practiced, she froze. It wasn't like Jana not to be able to dance. Dancing was her life! The teacher knew right away that something wasn't quite right. So, as she watched the other girls dance, she thought about what she should do. She asked Jana to see her after class and they would talk.

Once class was over, and Jana changed into her regular clothes, she walked over to Mrs. Berry, the teacher. At first, Jana thought she was in trouble. She believed that Mrs. Berry must have thought Jana didn't practice at all during the week. When really, that was not at all what happened.

As the teacher began to speak, Jana realized she wasn't in trouble. Mrs. Berry showed concern about something else being wrong. She didn't doubt for a minute that Jana had worked hard the last few days; she was just worried about her.

During their visit, Jana told her about the math test coming up. She also said that she was afraid if she didn't do well, her mother might take dance class away until her grades improved. Jana's mom had mentioned before that she should never allow dance to get in the way of school.

The next day in class, Jana was still worried about the math test. As she worked on her assignment, her eyes circled the room, and she wondered if any of the other students felt the same way she did.

As she looked behind her, at the students on the back row, she happened to notice something on the floor. It looked as if it had fallen off the teacher's desk, so she bent over to pick it up and return it to Mrs. Barnaby. As she did, she realized it was the key to the test! This actual real piece of paper in her hand had all of the answers to the math test she so dreaded having to take!

She looked around to see if anyone had noticed her with the paper. Everyone was busy working, including the teacher. What a chance she had! Jana held the answer to every test question in her hands and no one even knew it! Her first thought was to open her notebook and place it very neatly inside as if it were her own.

So, she grabbed her backpack and took out her notebook. The back pocket was the perfect place for this paper. If she opened it later in the day, in a different class, no one would see what was in the back pocket.

But, as she was about to slip the paper inside, something just wouldn't let her. It was not a person or a thing she could see or touch. It was something she was feeling inside.

It was a feeling she didn't like, and she wanted it gone. At that moment, she knew exactly what to do.

Because all the other students were still working, she got up quietly and went to Mrs. Barnaby's desk. She whispered and asked if she could speak with her outside about something very important. Of course, the teacher said yes, and she followed Jana to the hall.

As Mrs. Barnaby listened patiently, Jana began to tell her about what she found and what she was going to do with it. She explained that as she tried to cheat by stealing the paper that wasn't hers, her heart just wouldn't let her do that. For one thing, she loved her teacher, and she didn't want to lie to her. Jana said she would have been lying to her parents as well if she had taken the answers and cheated. She apologized for what she almost did and asked if she could take a different math test with different answers.

Because of her honesty, Jana prevented a major math mishap. She felt good about telling the truth and was willing to give up dance if it meant she was honest and tried her best. Even though she was under a huge amount of pressure to do well, she just *couldn't* cheat. That night, she studied as much as she could and hoped that tomorrow she would make a good enough grade so she could continue with dance class.

Right before test time, Jana thanked her teacher for giving her a second chance, and Mrs. Barnaby wished her good luck. She then sat down, took out a pencil, and wished herself good luck. Once the tests were passed out and Jana got started, she realized it wasn't as bad as she had convinced herself it would be. Studying the night before definitely helped.

Early the next week, Mrs. Barnaby had the tests graded and she passed them out to the students at the beginning of class. Many of Jana's classmates cheered out loud when they saw their grades. Jana was sure her grade wouldn't be good enough to cheer about…

As Mrs. Barnaby laid her test on her desk, she told Jana that the good luck wish must have helped. When Jana saw her grade, she didn't cheer, but she was surprised. She was happily surprised. She had earned an 83! Compared to the zero she would have gotten if she had been caught cheating, an 83 wasn't bad at all.

After school that day, Jana spoke with her mother about the math grade and told her about what happened the day before. Not only was Jana's mom happy with the grade, but she was also very pleased that Jana was so honest with herself and her teacher.

Then, she thanked Jana for telling her about it, and reassured her that she would be able to continue dance class.

Moral of the story:

In this story, Jana faces something called pressure. She was under pressure in more than one way. She had pressure to do well on the test, so she could continue dance class. She also experienced the pressure of almost doing something very wrong just to get a good grade. Jana did not give in to either of these pressures. Instead, she studied hard for her test so that she could keep dancing and chose to do the right thing by being honest about the test answers.

PLANET PRESENTATIONS

During science last Monday, Laura's teacher assigned a planet to each child. The instructions were to create a display of some sort that would show information and details about the particular planet. Open house was coming soon, and Mrs. Parker wanted the students' work to be displayed throughout the classroom. The planet projects would be great for the parents to see that night.

After the teacher told a few students what planet they were to research, she made her way to Laura's desk. She assigned Jupiter to Laura. Because she was more of a spelling bee type of girl, this planet business didn't interest her very much. She would rather be practicing how to spell words. To Laura, it didn't matter what the words were, she just wanted to know how to spell them. Ever since she was a tiny girl, letters and words had always been her favorite part of learning.

When Laura was a toddler, her mother had bought her several of those make-a-word puzzles, and she adored them. If she was able to choose a toy to take to the babysitter's house, she would take her puzzles. When she packed toys for vacation, she packed her puzzles. Mom always said that the puzzles were what started her love for spelling.

As a young girl who isn't so crazy about learning science facts, what was she going to do? She couldn't see herself in her room for the next two weeks, studying Jupiter. What could be so interesting about a silly planet? Don't we still have enough information left to learn about Earth?

By the time Tuesday night had arrived, Laura was still not any farther along than she was the day before. But when her dad came in to chat with her about things, he presented her with a new way to look at the project. He told her that for every new fact she learned about Jupiter, she could learn to spell some of the new words within that fact. He gave her an example: the word "temperature." As she learned about the temperature on Jupiter, she could practice spelling it as well!

After talking with Dad, Laura felt a lot better about things, and she also used his idea to come up with a presentation for the entire project. Instead of doing a display where she painted planets or made them out of clay, she would display the pieces of a classroom spelling lesson.

For the next several days, Laura worked hard to study and learn all she could about Jupiter. She made sure to make a list of all the new words she wanted to spell. By the end of the week, she had over 47 new words! She spent the second week designing activities and games that a teacher could use in the classroom to teach spelling.

On the day the presentations were due, Laura confidently walked up to the front of the class with hers. It was unlike anyone else's, but it did draw a lot of attention from the other students. As her turn approached, she stayed calm and reminded herself that even though she hadn't been familiar with Jupiter or anything about it two weeks ago, she definitely was now.

Laura proved to herself that even if she wasn't comfortable with something, there were ways of changing one thing into another. She wanted to remember this lesson for all the other areas in her life. She thought it would be valuable for the future as well.

With those thoughts still in her mind, she walked up to the front of the room holding her presentation. She showed the class all of the information on Jupiter that she had collected. Then, she presented the activities and games she had created to help teach spelling. Although her work was very different from the others, everyone loved it, including Mrs. Parker.

Laura earned a 100 for her planet presentation, and she also earned a 100 for her presentation skills. Her teacher complimented her for being very knowledgeable about the facts of her assigned planet, and she was very impressed that Laura turned it into something she enjoyed.

That evening at home, Laura was excited to tell her parents about her presentation and her grades. She also mentioned how proud the teacher was. She thanked her father again for giving her the idea. She assumed with the smile on both of her parents' faces, that they were proud of her too.

Moral of the story:

Being confident is important, and when you're confident with something it comes easier for you. Laura doesn't like science and wasn't comfortable presenting something about planets to the class. However, once she found a way to make the project fit her better, her confidence increased, and presenting it to the class was no big deal. She was aware that her project was created differently, and she was aware that it was not really what the teacher was expecting, but she was confident when presenting. That helped her stay calm and do a great job.

LOSING A BEST FRIEND

Liz sat, staring out the rain-covered window with sad eyes. She just watched her best friend, Tonya, drive away with her family to a new life. The two girls had been very close friends since kindergarten. Now that they were in fourth grade, they were like sisters. Not like the sisters that always argue, but the kind of sisters that are best friends.

Once, when they were both five, Tonya saved Liz's life. They were playing outside at Tonya's house and Liz fell in the pool. She tripped over a rock and fell in head-first. Tonya's parents had taken her for swimming lessons as a toddler due to the pool in the back yard. She was a very good swimmer, but Liz was not. As soon as Tonya realized her best friend was unsafe in the water, she jumped in and pulled her out. They were best friends before that day, but that moment made them like sisters. For years now, they've spent every weekend together either at one of their houses or at Tonya's grandma's house.

Tonya's grandmother was loved dearly by her family and friends. She was also the best baker in the area. She made cookies with sparkles in any shape requested, wedding cakes six layers high, chocolate candy that tasted like heaven, and muffins full of berries. Everyone came to her for any special occasion, and she was always busy. The girls loved to stay with her for lots of reasons, but one of the sweetest reasons was her pastries! She made all sorts of turn-overs, tarts, and stuffed croissants.

Tonya had lost her grandfather three years ago, and her grandma got lonely often. To help with that, she started baking. Because they were with her so much, Liz called her Grammy, just like Tonya did, and even if they didn't spend the night there, they would visit her most Saturdays. They would pick blackberries down the driveway, and sometimes, they would go fishing in the back pond. They both really enjoyed their time at Grammy's house and Liz wasn't ready to give that up. Tonya wasn't either, but they had no choice.

Tonya's dad had gotten a new job in Indiana. That was so many states away from Texas, and Liz knew there was a very good chance she would never see Tonya again. The night that Liz found out her best friend's family was moving away, she was devastated. She hugged Tonya, and they both cried for what seemed like hours. They spent the last three days together before Tonya left, trying to fit in as much fun time as possible.

Finally, the day arrived, and Tonya had to leave. Liz helped them load boxes and waved goodbye until their car disappeared in the distance. Every day, for weeks after she left, Liz sat at that same window and cried. Finally, one Friday evening, Liz's mother entered her room with a loud, "Guess what?" Then she added, "Somebody's moving in the house two doors down. That house has been empty, ever since that older man, Mr. Hudson, moved out last year. I can't believe we're finally getting new neighbors! I wonder who they are? Maybe they have kids around your age. You think?"

At that moment, Liz had no idea if they had kids, and to be very honest, she didn't care. She went to school every day, rode the bus, and didn't talk much to anyone anymore. Without Tonya, life just wasn't much fun. How could she possibly even try to think about new neighbors? Although Mom was just trying to help Liz, she found it bothersome. Before she knew it, she snapped at her mother with an attitude that was very hurtful.

Once her mom heard what Liz had to say, she told her she was grounded. Mom understood that her daughter was upset about losing her best friend, but she also knew Liz needed to control her emotions. If she was upset about

Tonya moving, she needed to know how to keep her feelings from coming out in anger towards someone else. As Liz thought about being grounded, she burst into tears. Not only was she extremely upset, but she was also in trouble!

At that moment, Mom realized that maybe Liz needed help handling her emotions. She sat down, hugged her while she cried, and told her a story about when she was a young girl. It started out when Liz's mother was six years old. She came in from school one day in a terrible mood. She stomped around the house for several minutes before she sat down at the dining table, put her head down, and cried big, heavy tears.

When her mother came in from the back yard, she saw her little girl having a meltdown, and of course, she was concerned. The very moment her mom stepped over to question what happened, Liz's mom stood up so roughly that she knocked the chair over backward. In an instant, she let out the loudest scream she could get out! Afterward, she began crying and sobbing.

Mom explained to Liz that she understood how little ones don't always know how to handle emotions, and parents are good at helping out with things like that. After they talked for a while, Liz began to feel a lot better. She could see her mother was right when she said that parents were good at helping untangle emotions. For the rest of the night, Liz was in much better spirits. She even helped Mom make chocolate chip cookies for the new neighbors.

The next day, she felt so much better that she decided to go with her mother to deliver the cookies to the new family down the road. They talked in anticipation as got closer to the house. As they approached the door, they could see toys in the yard and hear children playing in the back. Once Mom rang the doorbell, the door opened, and they were greeted with lots of smiles and hellos.

The family was kind and grateful for the cookies. The lady, Mrs. Tangelo, invited Liz and her mother in and introduced them to the entire family. There were three young children, all of which were much younger than Liz, but Liz thought they were all adorable. Mrs. Tangelo immediately felt comfortable and safe with Liz and her mother. She mentioned that, if it was okay with Mom, she may ask Liz to help her with the kids sometimes.

She was a writer and worked from home. She said that sometimes, she needed a helper to take care of the kids when her husband was at work, and she had typing to do. She explained that Liz could keep the children downstairs, entertain them, make their lunch, and play with them in the back yard. She also said she would pay her for helping!

All of this made Liz smile, and she told her mom as they walked back to their house that she hadn't smiled so big in several weeks. Liz really was beginning to feel better, and it was all because she was working on how to handle her emotions. Not only was she excited to make some extra spending money, but she also felt *so grown-up*! She had her first official babysitting job, and realized she had a lot to be happy about.

After all, even if Mrs. Tangelo would be right upstairs, it was still considered babysitting.

For the rest of the weekend, Liz thought about Tonya a little, but not as much as she had all the days before. Also, she didn't sit sadly next to the window. As a matter of fact, everywhere she went for the remainder of the weekend, she skipped there instead of walked. Her mood was improving, and her emotions were doing a lot better than they had been just a few short weeks ago.

The following Friday, Liz got her first chance to babysit after school for three hours. Mrs. Tangelo had some work due, and the children needed Liz's care. She cooked them a pizza in the oven, played mini golf with them on the back porch, helped with feeding the dog, and much more. As Liz cared for the kids, she realized just how much fun she was having.

She still missed Tonya every day, and every once in a while, she walked over to Grammy's for a sweet pastry and remembered the fun times they'd had there. Although, she wished she could see her best friend as often as she used to, it sure made it better having something fun to do with her time.

Moral of the story:

Realizing how to handle emotions can be difficult for young children. Lots of times, it takes an adult to help understand *why* you're feeling what they're feeling. Once you realize why you are experiencing certain feelings, you can work to get through them in a healthy way. Thinking and feeling healthy is just as important as eating healthy. This means, your body and mind both need to be cared for and treated well.

DINNER AT PAL'S PIZZA

Stacy had waited all year for this night! At school, she could hardly contain her excitement. Altogether, only 24 students were going. The bus wouldn't be crowded, and the students could sit anywhere they chose. She had a pocket full of coins and an appetite for pizza. On top of reading 100 books to earn this trip, she had made sure she had excellent behavior so she wouldn't lose it.

Back in August, when school first began, the second-grade teachers had a serious talk with all their students. They explained there would be a competition that would begin that very day. To earn the prize at the end, the requirement would be to read 100 books and pass a short test on each one. Each student had to keep up great behavior throughout the year, or they would lose their reward.

Stacy had done that very thing, and only 23 other students in the whole grade had accomplished that as well. Now it was celebration time! The reward was a trip to the bowling alley and game room across town. Afterward, they would stop for dinner at Pal's Pizza! As hard as Stacy tried, she couldn't decide which seemed like the most fun — bowling and playing games or eating and drinking all the pizza and soda she could handle! Pal's Pizza had 58 different types of pizza, three kinds of salad, lots of pasta dishes, and the best desserts around. She had only been there a few times, and each time it seemed like the food tased even better than the last.

When her big brother dropped her off at school, he gave her a few extra quarters for her pocket and told her to have fun. No one was as good at arcade games as her brother, and during the drive, he gave her lots of tips on how to move to the next levels on several of the games. As she grabbed her camera, Stacy told her brother bye, and ran to join the others on the bus. One of her good friends, Holly, was saving a seat for her. She plopped down, and they both began to giggle. The excitement was pouring out of them, and even when they had tried to hide their happiness, it wasn't possible.

Once all the students had arrived and everyone was seated, the bus driver was given the okay to head for the bowling alley. On the way there, Stacy and Holly played rock, paper, scissors and sang a few songs. The teachers enjoyed listening to them and even complimented their nice singing voices.

Pulling into the parking lot, the girls could see the sun beginning to set. The teachers stated that they would have two hours to bowl and play games. Because the pizza place was next door, they would walk right over after their time ended. Next, everyone exited the bus and walked in a line to the door of the Bowl-A-Billion, the best bowling alley and game room in the city!

As always, bowling shoes came first, then the choosing of the perfect ball. Some people did it the right way and chose a ball that 'wasn't too light or too heavy, but just right. However, Stacy wanted to choose by color. Quickly, she realized choosing the best ball according to its weight was actually the best way. So, she got her mind off the aqua blue one, and tried to find one she could lift. She finally found one that seemed like a good weight, but it was dark red, which wasn't her favorite. Still, her good attitude took over, and she made it work.

After a full game of bowling, the girls walked into the game room. They played several games, and Stacy tried to choose the ones her brother had given her advice on. She did make it to the seventh level on the wizard game he'd talked to her about. She noted that later, she would definitely need to thank him for his help. The other students were extremely impressed.

For the last half hour at the bowling alley, she and some of her friends took a turn in the tornado simulator and on the racetrack game where you actually get to drive a race car. After lots of fun with the games, the girls took a break and used a few of their coins for a drink at the concession stand. Overall, Stacy sure was having a great night, and they hadn't even gotten to the pizza yet! Along with all the laughs, Stacy knew she and her friends were making memories they would never forget. She was glad she'd remembered her camera because they took tons of silly pictures.

With only a few quarters left in her pocket, Stacy threw away her empty cup, and walked to turn in her bowling shoes once she heard her teacher blow the whistle. The students in second grade were very familiar with that whistle, and they knew exactly what it meant. At the end of recess each day, their teacher blew the whistle to call everyone to line up. If a child didn't start heading in by the first whistle blow, the teacher would do it one more time, but never a third. By the end of the first week of school, all students knew to be in a straight line, quiet, and ready to walk into the building. Everyone hurried to throw away their trash and get their shoes turned in, so they could get to the pizza even faster and wouldn't have to worry about the whistle.

They lined up, just like before, and walked out after the teachers thanked the owners for the use of the building. With just a few steps down the sidewalk, they were at Pal's Pizza, and boy was Stacy's stomach ready. Upon walking in, she could smell the wonderful scent of garlic, tomatoes, and onions. Italian food was her favorite, and pizza ranked the highest among her favorites!

In the parking lot before entering, the kids noticed more school buses outside. When they turned the corner, after grabbing their trays and cups, they could see the crowd that had been on those buses. It was no big deal that other schools were there at the same time that her school was. Pal's always had great service, and they were known for how well they kept the counter stocked with fresh pizza pies!

Except that night, they were a worker short, and they were struggling to keep the counter stocked with everything they offered. As Stacy took her plate to fill it up, she overheard someone behind her complaining that the pasta bowl had been empty for 10 minutes, and the soda machine was out of lemonade. As she reached for a slice of pepperoni, she heard someone else make a comment about how the salad bowl was nothing but carrots. They griped because all the lettuce had been taken, and they claimed the workers just weren't doing their jobs.

Stacy thought, *'how rude they are to stand just here and say those things. Can't they see the people are doing their best to serve us?'* After she made her choices, she sat down at the table next to her teacher and mentioned the comments she had just heard. Her teacher listened intently and praised her for recognizing disrespect. She took a moment to speak to the table about what the word respect meant. While the students ate and slurped their drinks, they all discussed it. Before everyone had finished, they made a plan to thank the workers by cleaning up their own mess. The students made sure not to leave much for them to worry about after they had left.

Stacy thought that was a great idea, but she wanted to do something more. She really felt they should tell the workers how she and her classmates appreciated their effort. All through the hurtful complaints and mean looks from the other customers, each server had stayed calm and pleasant as they provided dinner for everyone. Not only did the workers show great character, but they also showed respect in a moment when it must have been very hard for them to show it.

So, before the group left, Stacy made her way to the serving counter and spoke to one of the workers. She told them how she felt and that her teacher and classmates felt the same way. They thanked her for being so kind and told her they wished all customers could be as thoughtful as her.

Moral of the story:

A young girl notices disrespect. She considers why it's wrong and decides to do something about it. She learns that even when someone is being disrespectful, you can be helpful by not joining in the disrespect. She also realizes that she can help turn around the situation by making sure she always shows respect no matter where she is or what she is doing.

MOLLY'S SPEECH

Third grade was turning out to be the most fun year ever for Molly! She had made several new friends, she'd mastered every routine in dance class this year, and every day, she saw her hard work paying off with extra good grades in spelling.

Mrs. Rosen, her teacher, seemed to be extremely proud of Molly. Each time she got a graded paper back, there was a smiley face or a sticker next her grade, and Mrs. Rosen was always pleased with Molly's spelling tests.

Every Friday, when her class took a spelling test, Molly made a 100, and she always got the five extra points from the bonus word. The hardest bonus word she'd ever had was the word "circumference." That is the word for the distance all the way around a circle. For that word, her teacher gave her seven extra points!

One morning about two weeks before school was to be released for the summer break, Mrs. Rosen announced to the class that the academic awards ceremony would be coming up soon. She always gave the basic awards such as a certificate for all A's and B's, and she gave a gift card to those students who had all A's. She gave a P.E. plaque to the student who showed the most effort in P.E. class as well. However, this year, she told the class she would be adding something very special.

The new award would be called the "Best All Around" award. She explained it would be given to the student who not only had great behavior, but it would go to someone who was always helpful and had amazing grades. They had to have a good attitude and be respectful to everyone.

Mrs. Rosen said there were a few students whom she had thought deeply about as she was trying to choose someone to receive the award. She stated that she considered many things like those who had never missed turning in their homework and those who were always good listeners.

As the students chatted quietly about who they thought would win the award, the teacher wrote the next assignment on the board. While Molly worked, she thought and wondered if she might be considered for it.

Aside from spelling, she had earned good grades in all other subjects, was always kind to others, and worked really hard to be caring in all situations. However, there were other students who were the same in many ways. Molly had a good chance of being chosen, but she would have been happy for anyone else who received it.

The days went by, and the ceremony got closer and closer. With just five days to go, Mrs. Rosen told the class she would be announcing the student who was to receive the award at the end of the day. She explained that the chosen student would need to write a short speech and present it to the crowd during the ceremony.

That meant whoever received it would have four nights at home to prepare the speech. Suddenly, Molly wasn't as interested in the award. Who cared if she got it? What did it really matter? Molly knew she was a good student and didn't need a prize to prove it. As bad as she really wanted it—she didn't want to give a speech!

The day seemed so long, and all Molly could think about was how to make sure she DIDN'T get chosen. She considered breaking a rule like talking loudly during class or running in the hallway. She also even thought about not turning in her math homework.

Even though it was fully complete and ready in her folder, the teacher didn't have to know it was done. Hours passed, and Molly made her decision. She settled on the homework plan. As wrong as it was, she was willing to serve lunch detention to get out of the possibility of speaking in front of others.

Finally, math arrived, and when the teacher asked for all homework papers to be turned in, Molly didn't pass hers up. Midway through the class, the teacher questioned her about her homework, and she said she left it at home.

The teacher gave her a strange look, commented that it was unlike Molly to forget something so important, and went to her desk. At the end of class, as Molly was packing up, she dropped her folder, and all the papers inside came out and scattered around her feet. Her teacher was standing near and helped her pick up the mess.

Molly quickly tried to locate her homework paper before anyone else could see it, but she wasn't successful. The teacher picked it up, and with a confused look on her face, questioned Molly about the excuse she gave earlier. Molly was then forced to explain her concerns about the speech. Through tears, she told her why she was worried, and she apologized for being dishonest.

Afterward, the math teacher spoke with Mrs. Rosen and Molly in the hall. At that moment, Mrs. Rosen told Molly that she *was* the one who would be receiving the award, but she never meant for it to cause Molly to be so upset.

She talked with her for a while and went over all the reasons why Molly deserved the award. She promised she would stand with her as she gave her speech, and she even gave her some ideas to write about. Her encouragement began to help Molly see just how special the award was, and the overwhelming feelings of anxiety started to fade away.

During the next few nights at home, Molly worked on her speech with her parents, and prepared as much as she could. She chose the perfect outfit, and even made sure to lay out her lucky four-leaf clover earrings. Surely, with lots of practice, the perfect clothes, and luck, Molly would do fine.

On the day of the ceremony, that is exactly what happened. Molly was called up as the winner of the "Best All Around" award, and she walked up with a smile on her face and her speech in a folder. She placed it on the stand as Mrs. Rosen stepped over for support. She moved the microphone down to her level and began to speak.

The more she said, the easier it became, and before she knew it, she had read her entire speech and was finished. She had made it through the words from top to bottom and didn't make one mistake! After she was done and went to sit next to her parents, her breathing calmed, and she was able to enjoy the remainder of the ceremony.

On the last day of school, Molly gave her teacher a lovely gift of candles and soaps. She thanked her for a great year and gave her a hug. Then, she stated that she was very thankful she'd been chosen for the award, and it really meant a lot to her.

She also said that she and her parents were all grateful because Mrs. Rosen helped her get past all of the worries and anxieties that came along with it. Molly really did have a great third grade year, and now she was excited more than ever to see what fourth grade might bring!

Moral of the story:

Anxieties and worries may be difficult to deal with at times, but there are ways to overcome them. Molly, a young girl, was so overcome with fear of the possibility of speaking to a crowd that she was willing to be punished to get out of having to do it. She learned that through support from others, there is a way to work through your anxiety and be successful.

GARDENING GOALS

Every year, Mrs. Dunbar's science class was assigned a gardening project of some sort in the community. One of the spring projects was to grow a garden in the city park. The fruits and vegetables they grew were donated to the nursing homes and shelters in the area. Along with that, the group members that produced the best garden were awarded with season passes to the local theme park and museum.

Finally, it was Bethany's turn to do the gardening project. She loved growing vegetables, fruit trees, flowers, and all sorts of other plants, but she loved being in a competition even more! She was ready to show that she and her group could grow a better garden than everyone else!

Bethany was determined to get that theme park pass. If she were to earn that, she could get in any day she wanted, for free! What a magical moment it would be if the teacher called her name as the winner.

The day the project was assigned, Bethany was ready to begin. She sat with her group, outlined the plan, and began the written report that was to be turned in along with pictures of the garden. The group discussed the type of garden they wanted to grow.

There was a choice between a flower garden, a vegetable garden, all fruit trees and vines, or a mixture of any of those. They agreed that a mixture of all of these would be best because the flowers would bring in the pollinators to help everything grow and bloom faster.

As the team worked together to make sure every detail of their garden was perfect, there were a few disagreements and sometimes, even a clash in opinions. Out of the six members, three of them only wanted to plant the seeds.

They didn't want to have to help with the tilling of the soil. Others only wanted to do the drawings and make the plans. They said they had martial arts and gym classes after school, and there would never be time for them to help at the park.

Once everyone had a chance to speak their thoughts, Mrs. Dunbar stepped in to help with making arrangements for each student and their after-school activities. She created a list of duties for each person who couldn't participate at the park. In the end, everyone had an equal amount of work, and everyone was happy.

Although there had been some different opinions along the way, they all agreed on one thing for sure — they all wanted theme park passes!

Luckily, the park was right across the street from the elementary school, and during the following days, all seven groups worked to their best ability to make their ideas come to life. They mapped out their allotted areas, gathered tools and gloves, and brought plenty of water bottles to help with the hot afternoons. Buckets of soil and fertilizer were carried in, and wheelbarrows full of mulch were lined up near the footbridge.

Sprouts of green beans, tomatoes, and cantaloupe were stationed by the creek's edge, and packets of seeds were piled high in Mrs. Dunbar's wagon. The air was full of early visitors, and it seemed like the bees and butterflies were already noticing their work.

The teacher walked around and inspected everyone's work. She noticed how some students were getting along nicely while others were spending their time arguing. As she stopped and visited with the groups, each student explained their part in the work.

When she came to Bethany, she told her teacher that her part was to dig the holes to plant the potatoes, decide which flower seeds to plant, and to keep the rows separated by weeding. She also said that she would water the garden on Mondays, Tuesdays, and Fridays. The other members of her group explained their parts to Mrs. Dunbar, and she walked away pleased.

Bethany's group talked and all agreed that they seemed to be working very well together. They decided that as long as they stuck to their word and completed their assignments, their garden would be amazing in the end.

As a group, they walked around the park and inspected others' gardens. They made sure to compliment the other group's work as they passed by. They noticed how some made their gardens in different shapes such as a hexagon shape or a diamond shape. They also saw some students working as partners instead of each person having individual jobs. Overall, they saw lots of things that were different from their ideas, but they knew their group had a good plan and a good chance of winning. They stuck to their mission, kept their jobs the same, and continued working toward their goal.

On the morning the winner was supposed to be announced, the class found that one of the gardens had been destroyed.

It was a garden full of flowers and vegetables, and only the vegetables had been dug up, nibbled on, and tossed about.

The flowers were still standing, so Mrs. Dunbar assumed that some type of critter had enjoyed the vegetables for last night's dinner. It was a sad moment for that group who had worked hard to make it look so nice.

After taking a few notes in the grade book, Mrs. Dunbar explained that because they didn't have a complete garden, they were no longer in the competition for the theme park passes, but they had still earned 100s for their grades.

While the teacher continued to examine the gardens, their contents, and the physical work that had been put into each one, she took notes and finally made a decision. She announced, after much consideration, that the winner was Bethany's group. They had done it! They had reached their goal. With all their hard work, determination, and skills, they had won the competition and earned the passes to the theme park!

However, they discussed things and how that other garden had got ruined. Afterward, they decided to accept the honor of growing the best garden, but they gave their theme park passes to the students who had lost their chance at winning them.

Among the seven team members, they all agreed they had reached their goal of producing the most fabulous garden and winning the passes. They also agreed the happiness they had for reaching their goal far outweighed going to the theme park. It made them much happier to present the passes to their friends.

In the end, the teacher was able to send a story to the local newspaper about two winning teams instead of just one as in the years past. She was excited that her students had not only worked well together as small groups, but they also worked as a team overall. It was a great day for all the students, but it was an amazing day for Mrs. Dunbar!

Moral of the story:

The teams in this story all worked hard to reach their goals. In the beginning, Bethany's team knew it would take persistence and working together to reach their goals. They stayed on track and earned what they were aiming for. However, they also learned that sometimes you may reach a goal you didn't even know you had. They gave their prize away to other students who lost their chance at winning. So, along with receiving what they tried so hard for, Bethany's group reached the goal of true friendship as well.

A NIGHT ON STAGE

Amy looked over the flyer for the upcoming play with anticipation. She had always wanted to be in a play, but she never had enough courage to try out in the past. Plays at her school were open to anyone throughout all the grade levels, and they had at least three every year. This time, the play was the wonderful classic, 'T'was the Night Before Christmas.' Amy loved this time of year, and she wanted more than anything to be brave enough to give acting a try.

However, on the day of tryouts, Amy backed out of trying out for a specific part. Instead, she just asked to work on the crew. Being a part of the play in that way was good enough for her first time. She carried props, helped with the lighting, and coordinated costumes for the actors. During the first four practices, Amy was completely satisfied and happy with her choice of jobs. She liked helping others, and the lighting tricks she learned were a lot of fun. Everyone was learning their lines, their places on stage, and how to speak loud enough for a large audience to hear.

As the weeks went by, things were really shaping up. The elves' striped socks had finally arrived, and the jingle bells for the reindeer were found in Santa's toy bag after being lost for 12 days. The children were working hard, the teacher was pleased, and everything seemed full of holiday perfection—until Mrs. Santa came down with a terrible cold!

Mr. Todd, the drama teacher, wasn't sure what to do when the actress for Mrs. Santa became sick. There hadn't been enough students at tryouts to have understudies. So, he did the only thing he could think of, and he asked the crew members if any of them felt like they could play Mrs. Santa. At first, Amy didn't even consider speaking up and volunteering for the spot, but after a couple of hours, it did cross her mind. Since she hadn't had enough courage a few weeks ago to try out, maybe she could now.

After all, she had helped Kristen, the girl who played Mrs. Santa, with her lines several times. Also, as she worked on the set, walking back and forth, and preparing for things to go just right, she constantly heard the actors speaking and rehearsing. So, even when she wasn't directly helping Kristen, she could hear her words from backstage. As a matter of fact, Amy had memorized many lines of several of the actors, not just Mrs. Santa's part.

The longer she thought about how many lines she really did know from all the different characters, she thought even more deeply about telling Mr. Todd that she wanted to give it a try. But, her lack of courage stood in her way, and she just couldn't do it. As she continued her job on the crew, another member, Amber, did take the challenge. Mr. Todd was very relieved that he finally had a Mrs. Santa replacement.

With only two weeks before the performance date, everyone was running around the stage like little Christmas mice preparing for the first dress rehearsal. Everyone, that is, except for Amber. She was the crew member who had taken over when Kristen got sick.

As Amy stood in confusion about where Amber could have been, Mr. Todd came running onto the stage in a panic. He told all the crew and cast members that Amber had been helping her parents decorate their front yard for the holidays, and she had tripped over a plastic sleigh and sprained her ankle!

With that news, Mr. Todd looked like he just wanted to throw his hands in the air and give up. Well, Amy certainly couldn't let that happen! Plus, the whole community was counting on this. The Christmas play was always the talk of the town, and if people found out it may be called off, that would make for one very sad Christmas time.

Before she could think too long and begin to second guess herself, Amy stood up and said she would take the part. She told the drama teacher that she knew all of the lines for Mrs. Santa. She also added she had never been in a play before, on stage in front of everyone, but she didn't want to let everyone down. Mr. Todd yelled, "Hooray!" and immediately got Amy into the Mrs. Claus costume. As the dress rehearsal started, Amy stood right in place and never missed a word. She knew all the motions to make, where to stand while others were talking, and every time she was supposed to smile. Mr. Todd was one happy and relieved teacher!

For the opening night, Amy wasn't as nervous as she thought she would be. With every dress rehearsal, she gained more and more courage. Five minutes into the show, Amy was already past being nervous and decided to just enjoy acting in the play.

She was happily surprised that courage had taken over and there were no more butterflies in her stomach. Throughout the play, the audience clapped, laughed, and seemed to truly be entertained. By the closing act, everyone was full of Christmas spirit and ready for Santa!

Moral of the story:

After Amy passes up many chances to participate in something she wants to do, she finds the courage to step up when she's needed most. She learns that all it takes is practicing and keeping your mind off being nervous to find your courage.

CONCLUSION

While growing up isn't always easy to do, there are valuable lessons to be learned in the process. Parents, teachers, counselors, and sometimes even older siblings can be a support for you in times of need. You can see from the stories in this book that each child had something particular to overcome, and they had to work to reach that goal.

You will have learned as you read that many times, it's hard facing new situations on your own, and sometimes it may be difficult to accept new challenges without knowing the outcome ahead of time. However, with the support of friends, family, and those around you, anything is possible.

You are an awesome girl with hidden talents you have yet to discover. As you grow, those talents will become obvious, and you will learn to use them to help you succeed. Accepting new opportunities can help you learn new things about yourself. Take time to find out what you're good at and use those results to help foster your wonderful personality.

During your life, there will be times when you are standing strong, and you will need to be the supportive person for someone who is in need. Always remember, no matter what side you're on at the time—you're worthy, you're important, and you are AWESOME!

Printed in Great Britain
by Amazon